A DK PUBLISHING BOOK

Senior Editor Susan Peach
Art Editor Marcus James
Editor Katherine Moss
Designer Jacqueline Gooden

US Editor Camela Decaire
DTP Designer Almudena Díaz
Managing Editor Jane Yorke
Managing Art Editor Chris Scollen

Dinosaur Consultant
Dr. Angela Milner,
The Natural History Museum, London.
Production Kate Oliver
Picture Research Sally Hamilton
Jacket Design Mike Buckley

First American Edition, 1997
4 6 8 10 9 7 5 3
Published in the United States by
DK Publishing, Inc., 95 Madison Avenue
New York, New York 10016

Visit us on the World Wide Web at
http://www.dk.com
Copyright © 1997 Dorling Kindersley
Limited, London

Published in Great Britain by
Dorling Kindersley Limited.

A catalog record for this book is available
from the Library of Congress.

ISBN: 0-7894-2051-1

Color reproduction by Flying Colours
Printed in Italy by L.E.G.O.

Photography by: Andy Crawford,
John Downes, Lynton Gardiner, Colin Keates,
Dave King, Tim Ridley, Dave Rudkin.

Armed to the Teeth

Horrible Heads

Tearing Talons

Suits of Armor

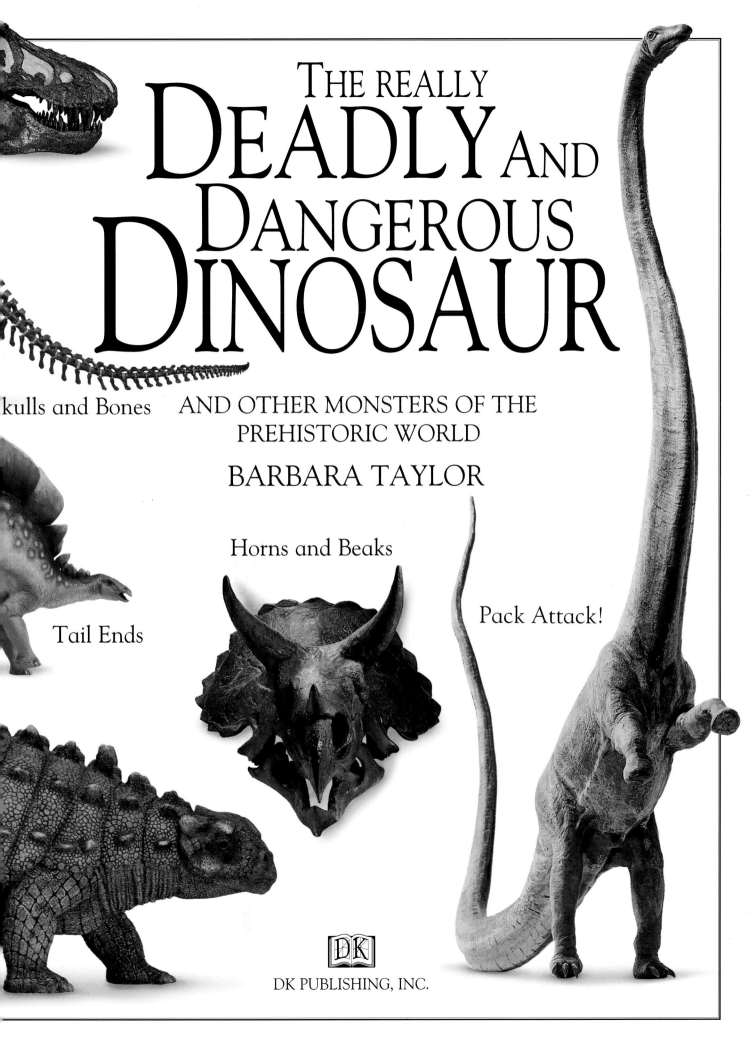

THE REALLY
DEADLY AND
DANGEROUS
DINOSAUR

kulls and Bones

AND OTHER MONSTERS OF THE
PREHISTORIC WORLD

BARBARA TAYLOR

Horns and Beaks

Tail Ends

Pack Attack!

DK PUBLISHING, INC.

ARMED TO THE TEETH

Meat-eating dinosaurs were ferocious hunters. They had sharp, stabbing teeth to kill their prey and then slice and tear flesh into chunks.

Tyrannosaurus's daggerlike teeth were longer than your hand. Their serrated edges cut through flesh like steak knives. Its jaws were strong enough to crush bones.

Tyrannosaurus

Giant saw-toothed jaws

Tyrannosaurus skull

Tyrannosaurus had huge jaws. It could have swallowed a person whole!

Baryonyx

The long snout was used to probe into corpses, too.

Baryonyx had a long head like a crocodile and sharp, pointed teeth to grip and seize slippery fish.

Rivals fought with their vicious fangs.

Compsognathus
Armed with small, sharp, curved teeth, *Compsognathus* snapped up small prey such as insects and lizards.

Tyrannosaurus may also have used its formidable teeth to stop a rival from stealing its food.

Plant eaters' teeth either cut or chewed.

Anchisaurus

Anchisaurus may have snipped off tree leaves or plants with its small, blunt teeth.

SUITS OF ARMOR

Hard hats, armor plating, spikes, shields, and a leathery skin gave these plant eaters a tough defense against even the fiercest predator.

A meat eater trying to bite through the bony chainmail and plates on *Saltasaurus's* back would probably have broken its teeth!

The bony plates were bigger than the palm of a person's hand.

Despite its size and heavy armor plating, this fearsome beast could lumber along pretty quickly.

Saltasurus

Edmontonia had a bony, hard hat and a spiky coat. It could have stabbed an attacker in the feet or legs with its long shoulder spines.

Edmontonia

This dinosaur even had bony eyelids to protect its eyes.

Euoplocephalus

Euoplocephalus was armor plated from head to foot. It had huge horny plates, bony studs, and a vicious tail club.

TEARING TALONS

Dinosaurs that hunted and killed other animals often had sharp, curved claws. They used these terrible weapons to hold and kill their victims.

Its stiff tail helped the dinosaur balance.

Deinonychus

The big, sharp toe claw was always ready for action.

Deinonychus leaped onto its prey, slashing with its daggerlike claws to rip open the animal's soft belly.

Fossilized *Deinonychus* hand

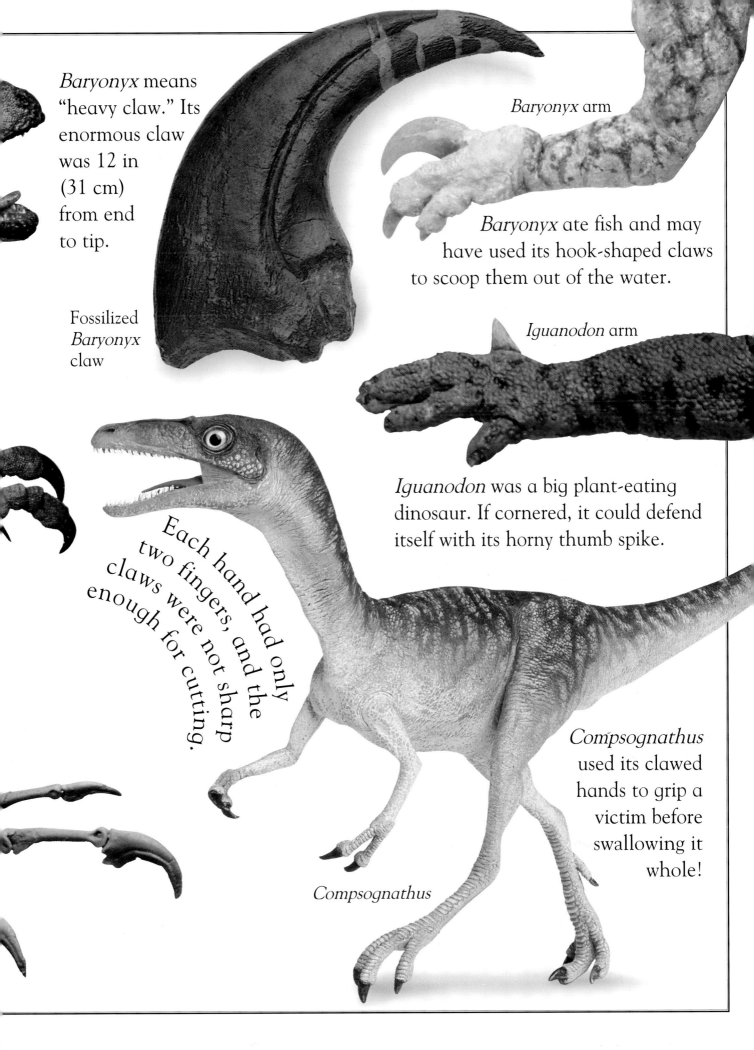

Baryonyx means "heavy claw." Its enormous claw was 12 in (31 cm) from end to tip.

Fossilized *Baryonyx* claw

Baryonyx arm

Baryonyx ate fish and may have used its hook-shaped claws to scoop them out of the water.

Iguanodon arm

Iguanodon was a big plant-eating dinosaur. If cornered, it could defend itself with its horny thumb spike.

Each hand had only two fingers, and the claws were not sharp enough for cutting.

Compsognathus used its clawed hands to grip a victim before swallowing it whole!

Compsognathus

HORNS AND BEAKS

Some dinosaurs looked rather like rhinos, but with frilly collars and parrots' beaks! They used their strange head armor for protection.

Although it looked fierce, *Triceratops* was a peaceful plant eater and used its beak to chop off mouthfuls of twigs and leaves.

Triceratops had ferocious horns to rip open the belly of an attacker, like this *Tyrannosaurus*.

Triceratops

This dinosaur's massive neck frill was solid bone.

Triceratops skull

The huge skull of a *Triceratops* took up more than a third of its entire body length.

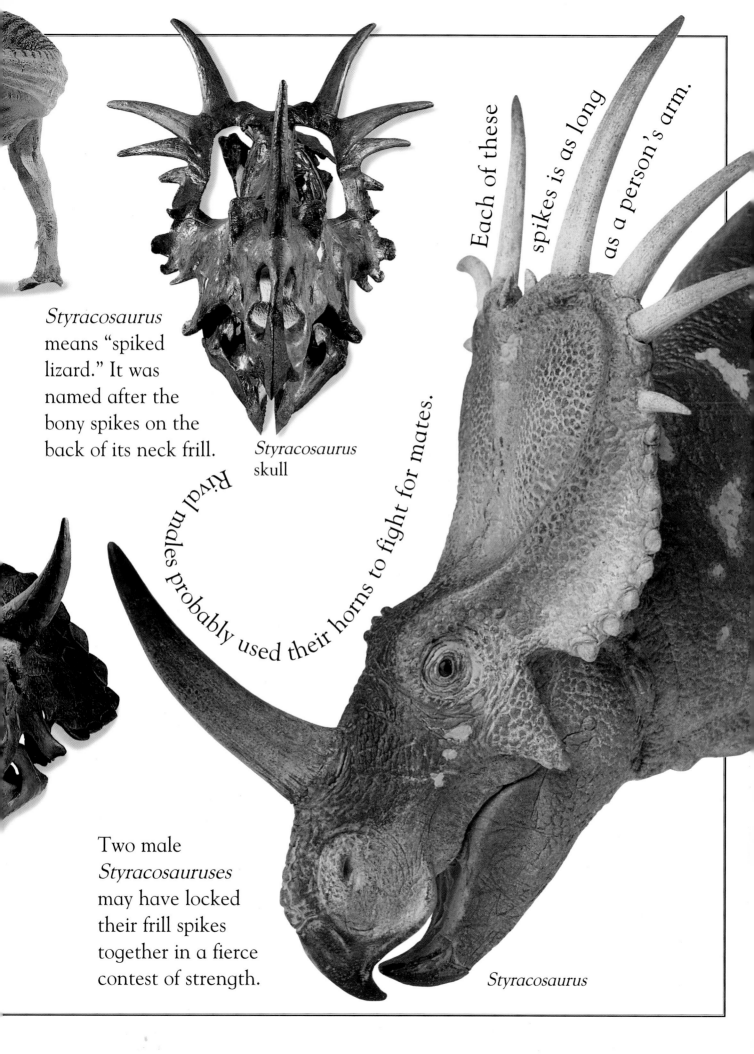

Styracosaurus means "spiked lizard." It was named after the bony spikes on the back of its neck frill.

Styracosaurus skull

Each of these spikes is as long as a person's arm.

Rival males probably used their horns to fight for mates.

Two male *Styracosauruses* may have locked their frill spikes together in a fierce contest of strength.

Styracosaurus

TAIL ENDS

Many apparently harmless plant eaters
had surprisingly nasty tails. A whack
from one of these dinosaurs' tail whips,
spikes, or clubs could
set the fiercest of
predators running.

Euoplocephalus

Swishing its spiky tail from side to side, a
slow-moving *Stegosaurus* could scare off predators.
The tip of the tail moved fastest and caused the most damage.

Barosaurus

By lashing the tip of
its tail like a whip,
Barosaurus could easily
beat off an attacker.

The long, heavy tail ended in a thin, whiplike tip.

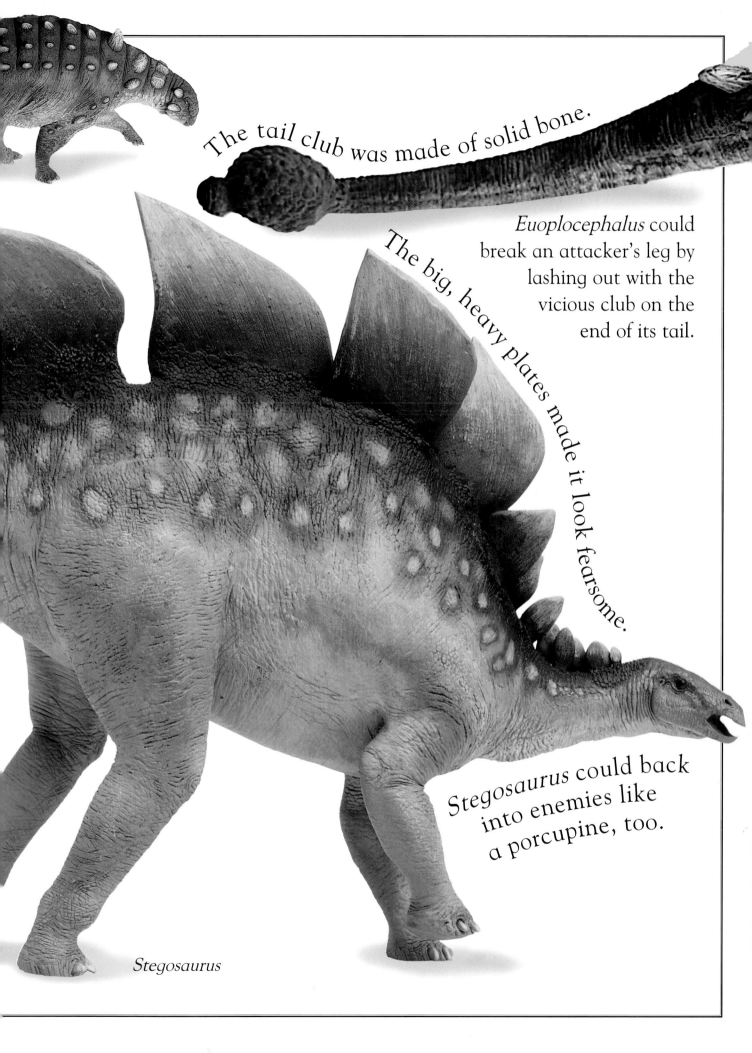

The tail club was made of solid bone.

Euoplocephalus could break an attacker's leg by lashing out with the vicious club on the end of its tail.

The big, heavy plates made it look fearsome.

Stegosaurus could back into enemies like a porcupine, too.

Stegosaurus

HORRIBLE HEADS

These dinosaurs used their weird head crests, helmets, and bony bumps to attract mates, make noises, or fight with rivals.

Troodon had two huge eyes at the front of its head, giving it expert vision and distance judgment.

Troodon

Stegoceras

Stegoceras had a battering-ram head for attack and defense. A built-in crash helmet helped protect its brain.

Dilophosaurus

Although the crest of *Dilophosaurus* was very fragile, it made it look like an enemy to avoid!

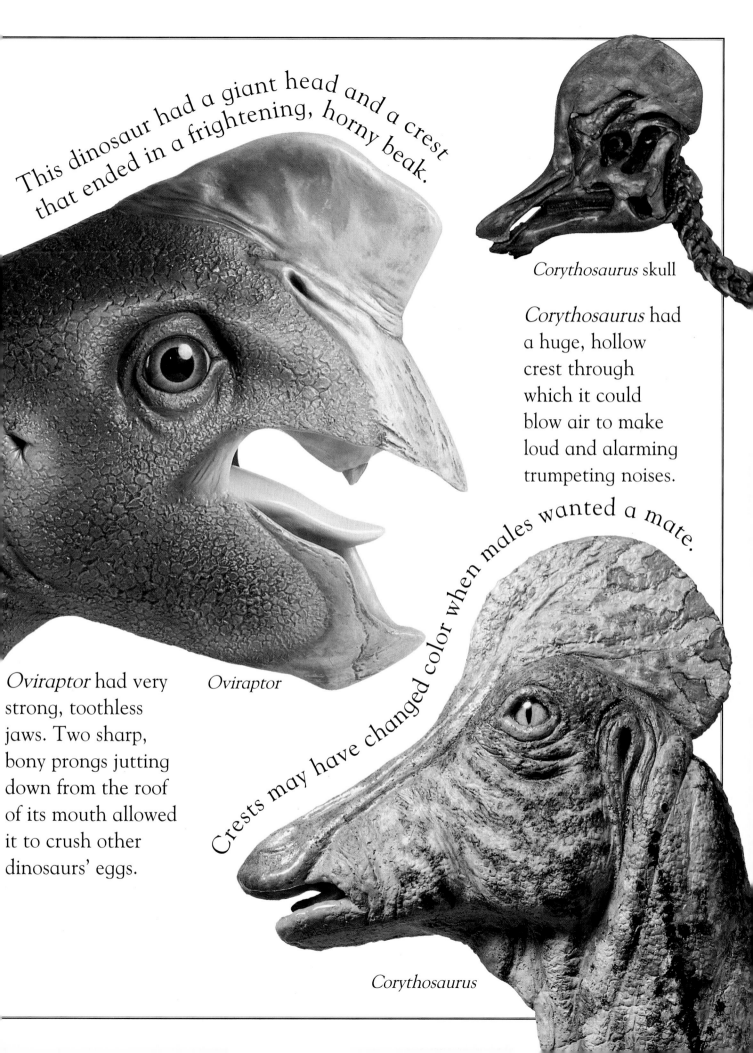

This dinosaur had a giant head and a crest that ended in a frightening, horny beak.

Corythosaurus skull

Corythosaurus had a huge, hollow crest through which it could blow air to make loud and alarming trumpeting noises.

Crests may have changed color when males wanted a mate.

Oviraptor had very strong, toothless jaws. Two sharp, bony prongs jutting down from the roof of its mouth allowed it to crush other dinosaurs' eggs.

Oviraptor

Corythosaurus

PACK ATTACK!

Dinosaurs were even more terrifying in packs. Some dinosaurs hunted in groups to kill large animals, while plant eaters often banded together for protection.

Corythosaurus herd

A pack of *Deinonychuses* may have attacked dinosaurs as big as this *Iguanodon*. Biting, slashing, and kicking, they ripped open their victims' bellies with their sharp, hooked claws.

Weakened from loss of blood, the victim soon collapsed and died.

At the first sign of a predator, a *Corythosaurus* would make booming calls to alert other members of the herd to the danger.

This fierce meat eater hunted alone.

Carnotaurus

Predators like *Carnotaurus* attacked plant eaters much bigger than themselves.

Iguanodon

Barosaurus was a harmless plant eater but could defend itself by rearing up on its back legs.

This dinosaur's long neck let it reach leaves on trees.

Deinonychus pack

Barosaurus

SKULLS AND BONES

It's amazing what you can find out from a few old bones and teeth! By reassembling these fossil clues, dinosaur experts can figure out how dinosaurs looked and lived over 265 million years ago.

A thick, domed skull shows a dinosaur fought with its head.

Stegoceras skeleton

From the fossils that have been discovered, experts have been able to build up an idea of the dinosaurs' shapes – we can almost see them in the flesh!

Grooves on the bones show the positions of muscles and tendons.

The toothless beak shows this dinosaur ate its prey whole.

Gallimimus skeleton

The long, strong shin bones show that *Gallimimus* was a fast runner. It could probably run as fast as a modern-day racehorse!

Tyrannosaurus's arms were too short to lift food to its mouth. Instead it probably lowered its huge head, bent its neck, and gnawed on a carcass.

Holes in the skull bones ensured *Tyrannosaurus's* head was not too heavy for its neck.

Tyrannosaurus skeleton

This dinosaur had a long neck to reach plants high above ground.

Riojasaurus skeleton

Big plant eaters, like this *Riojasaurus*, had thick, strong legs to support the huge weight of their bodies.